Contents

A load of rubbish

Until fairly recently, people used to dump all their rubbish out for the bin collectors and then forget about it. Not any more – thanks to recycling.

But how does recycling work and why is it so important? Read on and you'll find out, as well as getting loads of tips on how to do some recycling of your own.

Why is rubbish a problem?

People have been creating more and more rubbish – partly because there are more and more of us on the planet, and partly because we have more stuff than people ever had before. There are things to throw away now that weren't even invented a hundred years ago: plastic bottles, takeaway food packaging, mobile phones ...

What's wrong with throwing it away?

Years ago, people used to leave their rubbish lying around. This was smelly and unhealthy, but eventually it rotted away. Now, lots of things are made of materials that don't rot – plastic and polyester, for example. So we bury our rubbish, or burn it. But both these options can create big problems for the environment, and for people too. That's where recycling comes in.

What is recycling?

Recycling means making use of rubbish by breaking it down and turning it into something new.

Almost two thirds of what we throw away is recyclable – that is, capable of being recycled. In a few countries, people already recycle that amount but in most, people could recycle far more than they do.

Some things are recycled into the same kind of product all over again ...

or they may be made into something different but similar ...

but sometimes they're turned into something completely different.

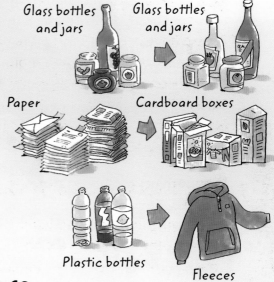

Glass bottles and jars → Glass bottles and jars

Paper → Cardboard boxes

Plastic bottles → Fleeces

Reduce and reuse

Recycling rubbish is much better than burying or burning it, but it's even better to reduce the amount you have to get rid of in the first place. Almost everyone can be less wasteful, by throwing less stuff away while it's still useful – and even by buying less too.

It's also better for the planet if we reuse things – by getting them mended, or giving them away for someone else to use.

Recycling and the planet

Recycling is great for reducing our rubbish mountain, but it's important in all sorts of other ways as well. Making recycled things causes far less damage to the planet than making them from scratch, and it costs less too.

Saving raw materials

A lot of our stuff is made from raw materials that come from the Earth, such as plastic and polyester from oil, electrical wires from copper, paper and wood from trees. It's wasteful to use up raw materials, some of which are scarce, when they could be recycled instead.

Most plastic bottles are made from oil.

Saving energy

The machines that make things and the machines that extract raw materials from the ground all need a lot of energy to make them work. This comes mainly from 'fossil fuels' – coal, gas and oil – which also have to be taken from the Earth.

Such huge amounts of these fuels have been used that it's getting harder to find enough of them to keep everything going. Recycling uses far less energy than making something brand-new, as the product has been processed once already.

Making a recycled drinks can uses only 5% of the energy of making one from scratch.

Recycling one glass bottle saves enough energy to power a computer for 25 minutes.

Saving the environment

The processes used to extract raw materials – quarrying for stone, logging for wood, mining for coal, drilling for oil – can all damage the environment. They harm wildlife, and create their own waste, which has to be cleaned up.

Waste heaps from mining can pollute the environment.

Fossil fuels have to be burned to produce energy. But the burning produces harmful waste gases. Some pollute the air and water. Others, such as carbon dioxide (CO_2), are the main cause of one of the planet's biggest problems – a rise in average temperatures, known as global warming. This is leading to climate changes, including more wild and dangerous weather.

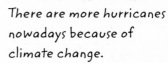

There are more hurricanes nowadays because of climate change.

Recycling also causes some damage to the environment but nothing like as much as *not* recycling. In fact, it would be worth recycling just to cut down on the CO_2 we produce, even if there were no other advantages to it at all.

Why not bury rubbish?

In some countries, including the UK and USA, most waste is buried out of sight in underground sites known as landfills.

What happens at a landfill?

A landfill is basically a big hole in the ground. The rubbish is tipped into it and then compactor trucks spread it out and squash it down to fit in as much as possible. Diggers tip soil around the rubbish at the end of each day.

Rubbish in landfill sites produces toxic liquids and climate-changing gases such as CO_2 and methane. The sites are lined with clay and plastic to stop the liquids leaking into the soil and polluting water that runs underground. Once the sites are full, they're capped with clay and plastic to stop the gases escaping into the air. Then they're covered over with grass.

Creating energy from landfill waste

Methane can cause 20 times more global warming than CO_2, as well as being smelly and explosive. But at some modern sites, it's put to use. It's pumped out of the landfill and burned to generate electricity for homes and businesses.

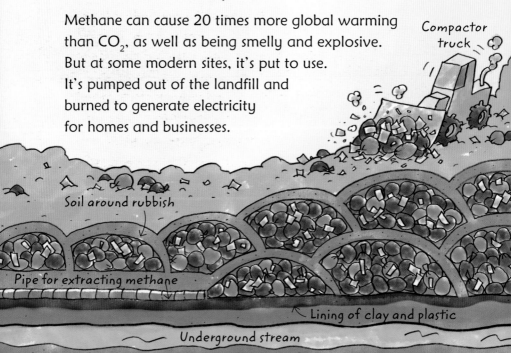

Compactor truck

Soil around rubbish

Pipe for extracting methane

Lining of clay and plastic

Underground stream

So what's the problem?

Even though the rubbish is out of sight and steps are taken to prevent pollution, burying rubbish isn't ideal.

* As we produce more rubbish, we need more and more landfill sites. It's getting harder to find enough land for them.

* Most of the rubbish won't rot away quickly, but will hang around for decades, for centuries, or even forever.

* Some rubbish will rot away fairly fast (see page 20) if it's in contact with air, but there's very little air in a covered landfill. And it's this kind of waste that produces methane, which escapes until the site is capped, or unless it's pumped out.

* In some parts of the world, landfill sites aren't lined or capped and, even when they are, they may eventually develop cracks.

* In an unlined or faulty site, soil becomes polluted. So does groundwater, which flows into rivers. The pollutants get into wildlife, food and drinking water.

* The slowly rotting rubbish gives off chemicals that smell like rotten eggs — not pleasant for people who live near the landfill site.

* If a site isn't covered properly, it attracts rats and flies, which carry disease.

Why not burn it?

Instead of being buried in landfill sites, rubbish can be burned in incinerators. This saves a lot of space in landfills, because only the ash left after burning has to be got rid of.

What happens at an incinerator?

At the incinerator, the rubbish is put in a furnace which is heated to a very high temperature. As the rubbish burns away, harmful waste gases are produced.

The best incinerators clean up the gases to stop them going up the chimney and into the air. What comes out of the chimney then is mainly hot air and steam.

Creating energy from incinerator waste

Incinerators can produce electricity at the same time as getting rid of rubbish. The heat of the furnace can be used to generate steam, which then drives a turbine to produce electricity. Although this is useful, much more energy can be saved by recycling than can be produced from waste.

What about the ash?

About a fifth of the weight of the original rubbish is left as ash after incineration. But it contains pollutants and needs to be treated. Some is then recycled as road building material, for example, and some is buried in landfills designed for hazardous waste.

So what's the problem?

Incineration can be a good solution but there are pitfalls.

* In some countries, laws on incineration emissions aren't always enforced. The waste gases may be belched into the air.

The gases can contain dioxins, which may cause cancer and are a type of 'persistent organic pollutant' (POP). Once POPs are in the environment or people's bodies, they're there for good.

The gases can also contain heavy metals, such as lead, which cause various illnesses, and dust which can lead to asthma and other lung diseases.

* Even in places with clean-up systems, environmentalists are concerned that too many toxins still get through.

* No amount of cleaning up can prevent the release of climate-changing CO_2, caused by the burning process.

* In some poor countries, rubbish is burned, not in incinerators, but in large, open dumps, and then the air gets chock-full of toxins.

* The ash still has to be disposed of.

How do I recycle?

So you'd like to recycle, but can't be bothered? Once you know how and what to recycle, you'll find it really isn't much trouble at all.

Where do I find out about it?

There may already be a leaflet at home from your local council, explaining how to go about recycling in your area. If not, you should be able to find out from the council website, or by phoning their recycling department.

Councils vary in the services they provide, but most pick up some stuff for recycling from your home. This may be with the rest of your rubbish, or on a different day.

What about stuff they don't collect?

To get some types of recycling picked up, such as garden waste, you may have to phone the council specially each time. Some things, such as old clothes and bedlinen, can often be put in a bin, called a recycling bank, in the street or a car park. And other stuff, such as wood or paint, may need to be taken to your local household waste recycling site. It all depends where you live.

If you have to deliver some recycling by car, it makes sense to drop it off when you're going that way in any case. Otherwise you'll be increasing the polluting emissions from your car, which will counteract some of the good of your recycling.

Do I have to sort it?

In some places you can lump all your recycling together in one container for collection. In others, you're asked to sort it out, often keeping paper separate from other materials. It depends on where your recycling will be taken to next.

It's important to sort things if you're asked to, or they may end up being buried or burned instead of recycled.

What do I put it in?

Your council may supply bins or bags for you to put your recycling in for collection, but it's easier to recycle if you get organized in the house as well.

There's no need for recycling to make your kitchen messy. You aren't creating any more rubbish – it's just that it needs to be stored differently. Once you're into the routine, you can massively increase your recycling rate.

You can buy double, triple or even quadruple bins for different kinds of waste.

If you're short of space, there are stackable bins too.

What can I recycle?

The list of things that it's possible to recycle is getting longer all the time. But some countries recycle much more than others. Germany, Belgium, the Netherlands and Austria, for example, recycle about two thirds of their rubbish. The UK and USA lag far behind.

What's recycled most?

Here are the things you're most likely to be able to recycle. You can find out more about them all later in the book.

* Glass bottles and jars

* Food and drinks cans

* Some kinds of plastic, especially drinks bottles

* Paper, including newspapers, junk mail, magazines and catalogues

* Cardboard, but not if it has traces of food on it. You'll need to flatten down any boxes. Greeting cards count as cardboard, not paper, and not all cards can be recycled (see page 18).

You'll probably need to remove the tops from glass and plastic containers and put them in with your normal rubbish.

Wash out bottles, jars, cans and plastics at the end of your normal washing up — if you use fresh, hot water you'll be wasting energy and water.
Squash cans and plastics if you can, but be careful not to cut yourself on cans.
There's no need to take off labels.

What's recycled sometimes?

It's becoming more usual for councils to recycle other things too. If you discover that yours doesn't do some of these, you could write to ask them if they'll start. A lot of recycling has begun as a result of pressure from the public and campaigners.

Depending on where you live, you might have to take most of these things to a recycling centre or a recycling bank, rather than have them picked up from your home.

* Food waste. Cooked food waste has to be dealt with in a different way from uncooked. See page 21 for more about this.

* Green garden waste, such as grass cuttings and prunings.

* Aluminium foil — kitchen foil, baking and freezing trays, takeaway and ready-meal containers. Wash them out thoroughly. Foil is often recycled to make components for cars.

* Aerosol cans, such as deodorants and spray cleaners. These need to be completely empty. Never try to squash them down or they might explode.

* Plastic bags — though it's best not to use them in the first place. (There's more about this later in the book.)

* Textiles — clothes, bedlinen, curtains, towels.

What about ...?

It's also possible to recycle these things:

* Cartons, such as soup and juice cartons. These are quite tricky because they contain a mixture of card, plastic and foil, which have to be separated. You need to wash them out before recycling.

* Mobile phones. These contain several highly toxic substances, but 80% of a phone's materials can be recycled. Many phone shops, charity shops and supermarkets run recycling schemes.

* Printer cartridges. Shops selling ink cartridges will often take your old one for recycling or give you a freepost addressed envelope to send it away in.

* Specs. Take your old specs or frames to an optician or charity shop that runs a recycling scheme. Your old ones may be just right for someone else. Some get sent to developing countries.

* Furniture — it can be broken down for its parts.

* Wood — it may be recycled into playground surfaces.

* Tyres. These are toxic if they're buried but can safely be made into sandals, pedals or bags.

* CDs and DVDs. These can be recycled into burglar alarms and street lighting.

* Cooking oil. This is sometimes converted into fuel and used to power vehicles and machinery such as generators.

The battery problem

Batteries contain highly toxic metals which can damage both wildlife and people if the batteries end up in landfills or incinerators.

In countries in the EU, battery producers now have to inform people how to return batteries for recycling. Electrical stores may have boxes you can put your dead batteries in.

See page 28 to find out about rechargeable batteries, which are by far the best kind to use.

What is e-waste?

Scrapped electrical appliances, such as fridges, washing machines, televisions and computers, are known as e-waste. They make very bulky rubbish, and contain lots of substances harmful to the environment if they're not broken down safely.

E-waste can be taken to council recycling centres. But in some countries, including those in the EU, shops have to take back appliances that were bought there, if you buy a replacement from them. The manufacturers then have to get them recycled so that their plastics, metals, glass and other components can be used again.

Out and about

Look out for recycling bins when you're out. If there aren't any, or you can't get your rubbish clean enough to put in them, take it home instead. Don't put it in a litter bin if you know it can be recycled.

What can't be recycled?

There are a few things that it's still difficult to recycle, either because the technology hasn't been developed yet, or because it costs too much. But this is improving all the time.

Can it ... can't it?

A lot depends on where the recycling is done. Some factories recycle envelopes with plastic windows, for example, but many can't. Before you put them in with your paper, check with your council whether you need to cut or tear out the windows.

Mostly unrecyclable

There are still some things that are mostly unrecyclable. They include:

* Anything that's dirty.

* Greeting cards, gift bags and wrapping paper with foil or glitter on them. The mix of materials is too hard to separate. It's best to buy non-foiled instead.

* Film plastic, such as clingfilm or magazine wrapping — it clogs up the recycling machinery and makes it break down.

* Broken crockery and some types of glass (see page 39).

* Crisp packets and chocolate wrappers — they may look as though they're made of aluminium foil, which can be recycled, but most aren't.

What do the symbols mean?

You can often tell whether something can be recycled, or has been made of recycled materials, because it will say so on it in words. But there are symbols to look for too, which make it easier to tell at a glance.

Looping arrows

Looping arrows are the most common recycling symbol. They're used all over the world.

The arrows show that a product is recyclable.

A number in the middle shows what percentage of the product is made from recyclate (recycled materials). If the arrows are on a black background, at least part of the product is made from recyclate.

This symbol also means that a product is recyclable.

'Green' symbols

Some symbols aren't to do with recycling but show that products are environmentally friendly, or 'green'.

This American symbol shows the product has been made to meet certain environmental standards.

This symbol doesn't mean that the product or packaging is recyclable. But it shows that the maker of the packaging has paid a contribution towards the recycling of packaging in general.

In the garden

If you have a garden, there's some waste you don't have to bother getting collected or taking anywhere. By composting, you can recycle it yourself right there, and do your plants some good as well.

What is compost?

Compost is natural fertilizer – it helps plants to grow but without the toxic chemicals that artificial fertilizers usually contain. You can make it from your biodegradable waste.

So what's biodegradable?

Biodegradable waste is waste that rots away fairly quickly if it's exposed to some air and isn't starved of oxygen by being buried underground. Food scraps (see opposite page), garden waste and paper are all biodegradable.

Where do I put this waste?

You can put it all in a compost bin or, if you have a big garden, make a compost heap out of it – but well away from the house to avoid smells.

Just give the stuff a stir occasionally and wait for it to rot down into compost over several months. Then spread it on your soil for extra-healthy plants.

You tip the waste into the top of the bin and take out the compost from the bottom when it's ready.

What can I compost?

* Fruit and vegetable peelings

* Egg shells

* Tea bags, tea leaves and coffee grounds

* Cardboard (e.g. toilet roll tubes, cereal packets, egg boxes)

* Paper bags and towels, unless covered in food; shredded paper

* Grass cuttings, prunings, small twigs and leaves

* Tear up cardboard and paper into smallish pieces, and mix only small amounts in with wetter stuff like food and grass.

* Don't try to compost any meat, fish, dairy or cooked food at home. It will smell, attract mice and flies, and spread disease.

Wiggly worms

To speed up composting, some people have a wormery. This is basically a special type of compost bin with composting worms that you have to buy. The worms munch through the rubbish, pass it out their other end, and so turn it into compost faster.

What if I don't have a garden?

You may be able to recycle your biodegradable rubbish even if you don't have a garden. Councils are getting better at collecting food and garden waste for recycling. Some even collect mixed food, including cooked as well as uncooked. Mixed food waste may be composted, but is more likely to be burned for electricity.

What's reducing all about?

Recycling is good, but reducing is the best way of all to cut down on waste mountains and help to protect the planet. But what does reducing involve?

Do I really need what I buy?

Everyone needs to think a bit harder about what they buy and why. Ads aren't produced just to let us know what's around. They're deliberately designed to make us want to buy things – and then the newest, upgraded version – even when we may not really need them, or be able to afford them.

Isn't buying recycled good enough?

It's true that making recycled goods uses fewer materials and less energy than making brand-new ones. So it's less damaging to the planet to buy recycled than unrecycled.

   But keeping what you've got for longer and cutting down on what you buy cause even less harm.

A good wash can make some things like new.

So how do I reduce?

If buying less doesn't sound like much fun, there are lots of easy and painless ways to cut down on waste, without depriving yourself of anything. Most of them can save you money too.

In the kitchen

* Take packed lunches in washable containers, so you don't use as much plastic, foil or paper wrapping. You can put smaller containers inside the main one for snacks like crisps or nuts.

* Most people tend to use more washing-up liquid, washing powder and household cleaner than they really need. See if you can still get things clean using less. It means you won't have to throw away containers as often. Also, many of these products pollute the environment when they're flushed away.

* Try to eat fresh foods in roughly the order they were bought, so they don't have time to go off.

* Don't throw leftovers away. Keep them in the fridge or freezer and eat them another time. Even a small amount can make a snack.

* Store leftovers and opened packs of food in washable containers. If there aren't any lids, cover them with plates instead of clingfilm or foil.

In the bathroom

* Try to cut down on toiletries. Besides reducing the amount of containers and packaging you throw away, this could be healthier for you too. Most toiletries contain artificial chemicals that get into your body through your skin or lungs, and some can be unhealthy.

* Always use up products completely before you bin the containers.

* Use less water, for example by turning off the tap while you clean your teeth and having a quick shower instead of a bath. The less water you use, the less has to be treated to make it safe. Water treatment uses energy and chemicals, and creates waste.

Saving paper

* Use the internet for writing to people. Send e-cards. And store photographs and documents on your computer.

* Write, draw, print and photocopy on both sides of your paper.

* Don't print out unless you have to, and use the draft/economy setting unless you really need a very high-quality print.

* Reduce the default margin and font settings on your computer so you can fit more on a page.

* Don't use kitchen roll or tissues to mop up spills. Use a cloth that you can wash out and reuse instead.

* Use a chalkboard or penboard, instead of paper, for writing messages at home.

Put recycling out.

Buying ...

* Look out for shops that sell products such as toiletries, cleaning products, or even food in refillable containers.

* Use refillable pencils.

* Avoid disposables, such as paper plates and cups, plastic cutlery, and single-use cameras. Besides, it's often cheaper in the long run to buy things you can use time and time again.

* Use low-energy light bulbs. Light bulb glass can rarely be recycled so it makes sense to buy bulbs that will last a long time. Low-energy bulbs last about ten times longer than ordinary bulbs, as well as saving loads of energy.

* Cut down on anything that can't easily be recycled, including foiled cards and gift wrap, and clingfilm.

* Buy products with the least packaging and refuse plastic bags in shops. There's more about packaging on pages 30-31.

* Buy someone a funky shopping bag for a present, so they don't need to use plastic bags.

... and not buying

* Share things you don't use very often.

* Download music and films to save on CDs and DVDs.

* Instead of buying a present for a relation, offer to help with jobs like gardening, car cleaning or decorating.

How about reusing?

Next best after reducing waste is to reuse as much stuff as possible. This means you can cut down on what you buy, throw less away and things don't even have to be recycled.

Make do and mend

If something breaks down, it's worth finding out if it can be mended. This can be cheaper than buying a replacement. You may even have a relation or family friend who can help – if they're good at carpentry, plumbing or IT for example.
   Here are some tips for making things last longer.

* If you learn to sew, you can take up or let down hems, sew on buttons, darn holes and mend tears.

* Some things can be mended quite simply – they may only need a splodge of glue. Never attempt an electrical repair without expert help, though.

* Check any batteries and bulbs before you decide something is broken. It could just be that these need recharging or replacing.

* Clean your shoes and get them re-heeled when they need it.

* Washing things can give them a whole new lease of life.

* If you have a bike, you might be able to fix it yourself, by learning basic bike maintenance – mending a puncture, raising the saddle, adjusting the brakes.

Junk or treasure?

You may think your old stuff is junk, but it's likely that someone somewhere will want it.

Charity shops are great places to donate to. They usually accept clothes, shoes, toys, books and games, as well as household items such as china. They may not take electrical goods in case they're unsafe, but they'll sometimes collect large pieces of furniture from your home.

What can I reuse?

If you'd like to start reusing as much as you can, you'll find lots of ideas below and on the next two pages.

Give, buy, borrow

* Shop at charity shops, second-hand shops and car boot sales, as well as taking your old stuff to them too.

* Ask your doctor, dentist, hairdresser or hospital if they'd like your old magazines for their waiting rooms.

* If you have a lot of plastic bags at home, ask if your local charity shop or greengrocer can make use of them.

* Use libraries and rental shops, as an alternative to buying books and DVDs.

* Swap books, magazines, CDs, DVDs and computer games with friends instead of buying new ones.
The swap doesn't have to be forever.
You can agree on a time to swap back.

Around the house

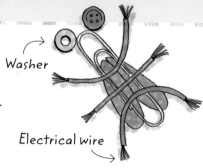

Washer

Electrical wire

An odds-and-ends bug

* If you enjoy making cards or other art and craft projects, you can keep a stash of old stuff to use — cards, magazine pictures, foil, wrappers, fabric, ribbons, tickets.

* Use old jars for storing odds and ends, such as coins, buttons, pens and pencils. You can also use old, clean jars for storing foods such as rice and flour, which will keep better that way.

* Use old spread and ice cream containers for storing leftovers. They need to be washed out very thoroughly first.

* Wash empty mineral water bottles and reuse them.

* Wash, dry and flatten foil so you can use it again.

* Buy refillable printer cartridges if you can. You can refill them at home using a refill kit, or some shops will do it for you.

* Reuse paper clips or use a stapleless stapler.

* Buy rechargeable batteries. They're widely available, include the word 'rechargeable' on the packet, and can be recharged in a battery charger up to 500 times.

* Old sheets are useful as dustsheets when you decorate.

* If they're not good enough for charity, you could tear up old, soft clothes such as T-shirts to use as cleaning cloths.

Paper, packaging, plastic

* Save cardboard boxes to store things
in, or for packing things you're going to
post or give to friends. Keep bubble wrap,
packing chips and padded envelopes for reuse too.

* If you open presents carefully, you can keep the wrapping paper.
Roll it up, so you can use it again.

* Cut the pictures off cards and make them into gift tags.

* Reuse envelopes – you can stick labels over the old addresses.

* Keep scrap paper for writing notes and lists.

* Offer big pieces of scrap paper, such
as wallpaper and newspaper, to nurseries
and playgroups. They may be able to use them for craft activities.

* Reuse plastic bags, even if only as bin liners or dog poo bags.

In the garden

* You could mix the fat left over from cooked meat with some
seeds to make a fat ball for the birds. See page 2 for where to find
a website that will tell you how to do this.

* An old bucket or tyre filled with soil can make a plant holder.

* You can use washing-up water and bath water
to water plants, as long as you haven't used
strong detergent or bath oils. It's best not to
keep watering the same plants with this
'grey' water though – share it around.

Going shopping

However much you try to reduce and reuse, you're still going to have to go shopping. Two of the best ways of shopping 'green' are to buy recycled products and products with the least packaging.

How can I cut down on packaging?

Some packaging is useful – it can protect goods or give you information. Too often, though, its purpose is just to make the product look good.

* Buy loose. Buy fruit and vegetables loose, not pre-packed. Some supermarkets have thin, compostable bags for them, but if you've only one or two items, there's no need for a bag at all. There's often less packaging at a greengrocers' or farmers' market.

* Buy big. There'll be less cardboard in a big box of cereal than in several small ones, less plastic in a big tub of yogurt than in several small ones. And you can always pour juice from a big bottle into a smaller, reusable one for when you go out.

* Look at packaging to see if it says it can be recycled or has the recycling symbols on it. If there's a choice of, say, an unrecyclable plastic bottle and recyclable glass, go for glass.

* Avoid ready meals – about 15% of the price goes on packaging, which usually gets too dirty to be recycled.

* Take bags with you when you go shopping, so you don't need to accept plastic ones.

Do you need a bag?

No, thanks.

Returning packaging

If you buy a big item with lots of unrecyclable packaging, such as hard polystyrene blocks or polystyrene chips, try asking if you can return it to the shop, after you've unpacked.

Some people are even starting to remove unwanted packaging and leave it at the checkout. The idea is that the shops won't like this and so will put pressure on the manufacturers to cut down.

What can I buy that's recycled?

As well as sending waste for recycling, it's important to buy recycled products, or the recycling will be pointless. And the more recycled goods people buy, the cheaper they'll get. Try to get into the habit of checking products and their containers to see whether they've been recycled.

It's easy to find recycled paper products, such as stationery and tissues, and recycled glass, including drinks glasses and even vases, but there are some more surprising things to look out for too:

* Sleeping bags stuffed with shredded phone directories
* Pencils made out of plastic vending cups or CD cases
* Beads made from rolled-up strips of magazines
* Garden benches made from polystyrene
* Writing paper from elephant dung
* Backpacks out of lorry tyres
* Carpets from plastic bottles

Soft toy made from old jumpers

Juice carton bag

Button eye

Where does recycling go?

Once you've dumped your recycling box or bags outside your house, thrown your shabby clothes in the textiles bank and taken your out-of-date printer to the dump, what happens to your rubbish then? Its story is far from over.

In the van

Some vans that collect recycling are divided into different compartments and the collectors make sure different materials go in the right one. That's why it's important to sort your recycling if your council asks you to. The collectors don't have time to go through and sort every item at the kerbside.

   Other vans have one big compartment for all the stuff, which then gets sorted later.

Where to next?

Your recycling gets taken to a materials recovery facility, known as a MRF – pronounced 'murf'. This is where unsorted rubbish gets sorted, and sorted rubbish gets sorted a bit more.

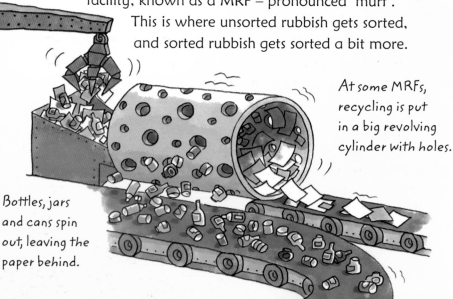

At some MRFs, recycling is put in a big revolving cylinder with holes.

Bottles, jars and cans spin out, leaving the paper behind.

On to the recycling plants

Once it's thoroughly sorted, your rubbish
goes to the factories that recycle different materials.
   Some of it may get sent abroad, which some people
say is bad for the planet, as transporting it there causes
pollution. Others say it's fine as long as the recycling
is packed onto ships returning from making deliveries
– that's better than having ships sailing home empty.

Does it really get recycled?

You may have heard reports about things sent for recycling
being found on rubbish dumps. This can happen.
   If, for example, someone puts food into a recycling box
meant for dry goods, a whole big batch can be
contaminated and then it can't be recycled. But if only
about 1% of a batch is contaminated, it's usually possible
for the recycling to go ahead.

Scavenging

In poor countries, recycling isn't always high-tech. People
may work for hours on open rubbish dumps, searching for
things that can be recycled. This is very bad for their
health if they have no protective clothing and
are exposed to dangerous chemicals – when
breaking open batteries, for example.
   But in many places, working
conditions are slowly
starting to improve.

Sorting the high-tech way

Materials recovery facilities, where recycling gets sorted, vary a lot. A MRF like the one shown here deals with pretty much everything except food. The rubbish comes in all mixed together, and is sorted on one giant, interlinked piece of machinery, which just keeps going and going.

The sniff test

The rubbish is tipped out onto the floor and someone has a good look and sniff at it. If food has got into it by mistake, it will stink and the whole batch may have to be landfilled or incinerated.

Next, the rubbish is picked up by a claw grab and dropped onto a conveyor belt. It goes through a bag-splitting machine, where the bags are ripped open so the contents spill out.

Separating the stuff

Next, the rubbish goes over some big spinning wheels. Most things fall through the gaps between the wheels, but large cardboard bounces over the top to get separated off.

Glass smashes into small pieces and falls right through to another conveyor belt at the bottom of the machine.

Spinning wheel

Cardboard

Follow the rubbish this way

Glass

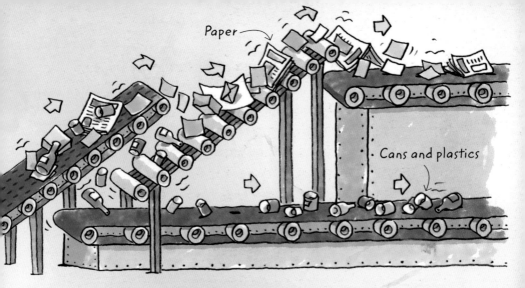

Paper

Cans and plastics

The rest of the rubbish continues over some more spinning wheels. Flat things, such as paper, roll up and over the top onto one belt, while solid objects roll down onto another.

The solid objects – mainly plastic containers and metal cans – pass under a series of infrared beams. The beams detect different types of plastic, and airjets then blow them down different chutes.

Metals continue along the belt. A magnet attracts the iron and steel, and electric currents pull out the aluminium.

Once the different types of waste have been separated, they are scrunched into bales and lifted off the ends of the belts by forklift trucks – ready for the recycling factories.

Sorting by hand

MRFs may be high-tech but they still need people. Once or twice, the rubbish passes through hand-picking cabins, where workers pick out anything that shouldn't be there – unrecyclable plastic, for example. This is dropped onto a different belt to be sent to an incinerator and burned for energy.

Pulping paper

In many developed countries, more paper and card is thrown away than anything else except garden waste. So it's especially important to recycle it, once we've reduced and reused as much as we can. One tonne of recycled paper saves 30,000 litres of water.

Where does paper come from?

Paper generally comes from trees in managed plantations, which means that new trees are planted to replace the ones that are felled. But trees take time to grow, toxic chemical fertilizers are used on the soil, and roads have to be made through the plantations. Also, tree plantations are much less rich in plant and animal life than natural forests.

How is it recycled?

Paper has to be sorted into different types mainly by hand, at the MRF. At the recycling plant it is pulped – turned into a soggy mush by being churned up with water. Any staples and sticky tape fall off at this stage, and chemicals are used in the water to remove ink and glue.

The pulp is sprayed onto a moving belt, where it passes between rollers which squeeze out the water. Once it's dry, the paper is wound into a big roll and stored, ready to be made into other paper products – from stationery to tissues.

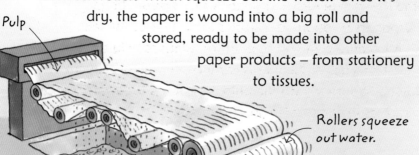

Pulp

Rollers squeeze out water.

Water tray

What's it made into?

Unlike glass, plastics and metals, which can be endlessly reprocessed, paper can only be recycled about five times. The fibres it's made from get shorter and weaker each time, until they become unrecyclable.

As the quality deteriorates, the paper is made into lower grade products. So top-quality office paper may eventually become newspaper, newspaper may be turned into cereal boxes, and cardboard may end up as toilet paper. Sometimes new paper fibres are mixed in with the recycled ones to preserve the quality of the paper for longer.

Once it becomes unrecyclable, paper can still be sent to an incinerator and burned as waste for energy. This is what happens to shredded paper, too – the bits are too small for recycling.

Unrecyclable paper can also be pulped, then spread on farms to improve the soil or shredded for animal bedding.

Why is some recycled paper off-white?

Some low-grade recycled paper such as paper bags, newspapers or phone directories look a bit off-white. This is because printed paper isn't always totally de-inked when it's recycled. Neither is cardboard. Instead, the ink is allowed to spread into the pulp. This saves loads of energy, as well as water and chemicals.

Crushing glass

Unlike a lot of rubbish, glass doesn't harm the planet by releasing toxins in landfill. But it doesn't decompose either. The earliest glass, made 3,000 years ago, is still found buried today. And glass takes a lot of energy to produce from scratch. So it's a good material to recycle – and can be processed over and over again without losing quality.

Sorting glass

It's important to sort your glass into different colours for separate recycling, if you're asked to. Once glass smashes into thousands of little pieces, it's very difficult to get the wrong colour bits out of a batch.

Some very modern machines sort glass using scanning cameras. If you aren't asked to sort yours, it may be because these are going to be used later. Or your glass may be going to be recycled as mixed-colour glass. This isn't made into new containers. Instead, it's crushed to make kitchen worktops or mixed with gravel for road surfaces.

You need to take off any easily removable bits of plastic or metal from your bottles and jars, including the tops and lids. These *can* be removed at the recycling factory but, if they slip through, they'll spoil the glass and may damage the recycling machinery.

Blue or black glass can sometimes go in with green.

Can all glass be recycled?

Some glass can't usually be put out for kerbside collection or into bottle banks. But you may be able to take it to your local recycling centre instead. This includes glass cookware or tableware – bowls, drinking glasses or jugs, for example; sheets of glass, such as mirrors or windows; and light bulbs.

How is it recycled?

As the glass goes past on a conveyor belt, workers check that it's been sorted correctly and take out anything that isn't glass, such as bits of plastic.

Next, the glass is washed by strong water jets – this is when the labels come off. Then, heavy rollers crush it into tiny pieces, called cullet. Metal detectors take out any pieces of metal, and vacuums suck up scraps of paper. The cullet is heated in a furnace so it melts and then it's shaped into new bottles and jars.

Facts and figures

* Recycling one bottle, instead of making one from scratch, saves enough energy to power a television for 20 minutes.
* A bottle sent for recycling can be back on the supermarket shelves in less than three weeks.
* In Switzerland and Finland, more than 90% of glass bottles and jars are recycled.

Is plastic a problem?

Plastic is a really useful material – it can be made in any shape or colour, and it's lightweight and hardwearing. In fact, it's so practical that we use 20 times more of it than people did 50 years ago, when it first became widely available.

So what's the catch?

* No one knows how long discarded plastic will take to rot away because it hasn't been around for long enough to tell. Scientists think it will take thousands of years – or even forever.

* Plastic releases a lot of CO_2 when it's incinerated.

* Some plastic can release harmful dioxins when it's incinerated.

* Most plastic is made from oil and almost a tenth of the world's annual oil supplies are used up in its manufacture.

* It often contains toxins, which can get into people's bodies through their noses, mouths or skin. The toxins include POPs (see page 11).

* A huge amount of plastic rubbish gets dumped, blown or washed into the world's oceans, where it pollutes sea life – and our seafood.

Can all plastic be recycled?

All plastic is recyclable, but it has to be sorted into seven different types, which all have to be processed differently. Recycling symbols are stamped into the plastic, but you may have to look quite hard to find them.

This symbol shows the plastic is type 1 and made from 'PET' (polyethylene terephthalate). Look for it on drinks bottles.

1
PET

From bottle to fleece

The way plastic gets recycled depends on its type and what it's going to be made into. But basically it's chopped up, melted down and reshaped – sometimes in a surprising way.

To make plastic bottles into fleeces, the bottles are first sorted into types and colours, either by hand or machine, and are washed by strong water jets. Then they're torn into bits by spiky rollers and the bits are heated until they melt. The melted plastic is pushed through holes to make long strands. When the strands have cooled, they're woven into fabric. It takes about 25 two-litre bottles to make an adult's fleece.

Melted plastic is turned into strands.

'Green' plastics

Plastics are becoming more environmentally friendly. Some modern plastics even biodegrade and so can be composted. Look out for plastic bags marked 'biodegradable'.

There are also plastics that photodegrade – decompose when exposed to light. But it can be hard to achieve just the right conditions for this to happen.

Experts have high hopes of the latest plastics, made not from oil but from plants. Some of these 'bio-plastics' even dissolve in water. Also, bio-plastics don't require the dangerous chemical additives that other plastics do.

Some bio-plastics are useful for toys, which may be sucked.

Melting down metals

It's fairly easy to recycle metals. The technology is very advanced, and the quality of the metals doesn't deteriorate, however many times they're reprocessed. Aluminium and steel – used in cars, computers and buildings, as well as food and drinks cans – are the metals most often recycled.

How are aluminium cans recycled?

Aluminium is used to make 75% of drinks cans. Used cans arrive at the recycling plant crushed and packed into bales. First, they're shredded into bits. Then, hot air is used to burn off any patterns or logos. Next, the bits are heated until they melt. The melted metal is poured into moulds, where it's left to cool into solid blocks. The blocks are ironed into sheets, so new cans can be made from them.

The blocks of metal can be so big that one block makes more than a million new cans.

Metal facts and figures

* Recycling one aluminium drinks can saves enough energy to power a television for three hours.
* If you bin two aluminium cans, you waste more energy than many people in developing countries each use in a day.
* Recycling steel cans produces only 20% of the CO_2 of making them from scratch, while recycling aluminium cans produces only 5% of the CO_2.
* In Brazil, almost 100% of aluminium cans are recycled.

What to do with textiles?

Natural fabrics, such as cotton and wool, produce methane while they're rotting in landfill, and synthetic fabrics, such as polyester, rot just as slowly as plastic. So it's as important to recycle clothes and linens as other things.

What happens to textiles?

Over two thirds of textiles put into textiles banks are reused rather than recycled. They're sent for people in developing countries or given to the homeless.

But if the quality is too poor for reuse, they can be recycled. They're usually made into cleaning cloths for use in factories, or stuffing for mattresses and cushions, although some fashion designers are starting to make recycled clothes.

How are they recycled?

Textiles are sorted by hand into type and colour. There are dozens of different types and the sorters have to be able to spot them in seconds as they go by on a conveyor belt.

After sorting, the textiles are shredded into fibres of the sort they were originally made from. These fibres are known as 'shoddy'. The shoddy can then be spun, ready for weaving or knitting into new things.

If something like a rug is being made, some brand-new fibres may be blended in with the shoddy to improve the quality.

The future of rubbish

As technology gets more advanced, new ways of dealing with waste are always being developed. So does this mean we won't have to worry about our rubbish in the future?

Waste technology

It's already possible to turn waste into energy by harnessing landfill gas or incinerator steam to produce electricity, or by using cooking oil to make engine fuel. In the future, perhaps it will be possible to get rid of all our waste without causing any damage to the planet.

But the volume of waste being created is still increasing and, no matter how efficient we get at disposing of it, there'll still be problems. As long as so many brand-new things continue to be made, we'll still be using up raw materials, wasting energy and damaging the environment.

Paying to get rid of rubbish

Most people pay for their rubbish collection through their taxes. But it's going to become more common to 'pay as you throw' – that's by number of bags or by weight. This should persuade us to cut down, and to recycle more.

In some places, people are encouraged to recycle because they get fined if they don't, or are paid if they do. In a town in Brazil, people even get food in exchange for recycling.

In Denmark, people pay extra for bottles. They get it back if they return the bottles to a bottle bank.

Green design

Manufacturers are starting to think harder about the effect their products have on the planet. As governments put pressure on them to take more responsibility for the waste they create, they're more likely to make things that are repairable, easily recyclable, and last longer in the first place.

This symbol means the makers of the product have minimized damage to the environment during manufacture.

Towards a new lifestyle

Our current way of life – including buying so much stuff and soon throwing it away – just isn't sustainable. That means it can't continue without damaging the planet beyond repair for future generations.

But recycling rates have increased generally over the last few years and there are some big changes going on. For example, in Sweden it's now illegal to put biodegradable waste in landfills, and in Bangladesh plastic bags have been banned throughout the whole country.

Reducing, reusing and recycling aren't all that are needed to save the planet – there's a lot else to do too. But they are a huge step towards a more sustainable lifestyle – and everyone can play a part.

Reduce, reuse, recycle

Glossary

biodegradable waste – waste that rots naturally. It does this fairly fast if it's exposed to some air. It's organic waste (see page 47) that is biodegradable.

bio-plastics – plastics made from plant oils or sugars, rather than from crude oil (see below).

carbon dioxide (CO_2) – a gas produced when people and animals breathe out, when things are burned, and when biodegradable rubbish rots. It's made of two parts oxygen and one part carbon.

climate change – changes to the typical weather conditions in a particular place.

compost – biodegradable waste that has rotted and can be spread on soil to improve its quality.

crude oil – oil extracted from the ground that hasn't yet been processed.

environment – surroundings, including the landscape, air and living things.

e-waste – discarded electrical or electronic goods.

fossil fuel – a fuel such as coal, oil or natural gas, formed from the rotted remains of prehistoric plants or animals.

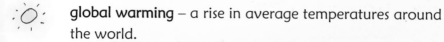

global warming – a rise in average temperatures around the world.

methane – a gas produced when biodegradable rubbish rots without air, and by farm animals and growing rice.

MRF (pronounced 'murf') – short for materials recovery facility, where waste is sorted before it's recycled.

organic waste – waste that comes from things that were once alive, such as plants or animals.

pollution – harmful waste or dirt that builds up faster than it can be broken down.

recyclable – capable of being recycled.

recyclate – material that has been recycled.

recycling – making used materials reusable by treating them in various ways.

sustainable – using only the amount of the planet's resources that is possible without damaging it for future generations.

toxins – poisons and pollutants.

waste hierarchy – the ways in which waste can be dealt with, listed from best to worst: reduce, reuse, recycle, waste to energy, incineration, landfill.

waste to energy – any process used to produce energy from rubbish, such as harnessing the power released by incineration to create electricity.

Index